THE TRADITIONAL DANCES OF LATIN AMERICA

DANCES OF MEXICO

General Editor

W. O. GALBRAITH

Technical Editor

JOAN WILDEBLOOD

Plate 1 *Los Viejitos*

Dances of MEXICO

GUILLERMINA DICKINS

NOVERRE PRESS

Contents

INTRODUCTION	5
Music	6
The Concheros	7
Regional Dances	8
THE DANCES	11
La Sandunga	11
Los Viejitos	22
Jarabe Tapatío	30
BIBLIOGRAPHY	44

Music arranged by Guillermina Dickins
Illustrations by Mireya Iturbe

The author wishes to express her sincere thanks to Maestro Géronimo Baqueiro Foster, for his helpful comments and for so generously putting his extensive library at her disposal for valuable source-material; to Sra. Mireya Iturbe for the original illustrations; and to M. Stefan Bobek for his kind help.

First published in 1954
This edition published in 2021 by
The Noverre Press
ISBN 978-1-914311-1-35-2
© 2021 The Noverre Press

Introduction

Mexico is fortunate in having a rich variety of dances, music, and costume, preserving an ancient heritage. Dancing has flourished since the days of the Aztec pyramid builders, and was performed to reflect the religious, spiritual, and emotional experiences of the people's lives.

The Aztecs had their *cuicalli* or *cuicacuilli* (houses of song and dance) near their temples, which were dedicated to the god of music and dance, Macuilxochitl, 'five flowers'; also known as Xochipilli, 'he who gives flowers'. Here lived the teachers who devoted themselves to instructing the young people from the age of twelve upwards, who were punished if they failed to attend. The women had their separate dances, but occasionally danced with the men.

The arts of music and dance were necessary for every religious and secular festival, as well as for the practice of magical rites. The dance was divided into the 'big' and 'little' dances, most of which were accompanied by singing. The 'big' dances were performed in the inner court of the chief temple, or in the main plaza. The 'little' dances were given in private fiestas for nobles, or at home for weddings or other celebrations.

According to the historian Durán, the favourite dance of the Mexican was the beautiful dance performed in honour of Huizilopochtli, the god of war. In an arbour of roses in the temple of the god, sat a woman, representing Xochiquetzalli, the goddess of beauty, love and flowers, surrounded by dancers adorned with roses. In nearby artificial trees, filled with fragrant roses, little boys dressed brilliantly as birds and butterflies jumped from branch to branch, sipping the nectar of the flowers. When the men, dressed as gods, came out of the temple and pretended to kill the birds, Xochiquetzalli appeared and led the men into her rose arbour, seating them near her and according them the respect and honour due to the gods they represented.

Music

As often happens with warrior people, percussion instruments came first in the evolution of their music. To the beat of the drums and the rattle of the gourds, these primitive people learned their ceremonial dances. The Aztecs played their melody on the *tlapitzalli* or ocarina; the *chililihtli* or flute; and the *atecocolli* or caracol, which was similar to the cornamusa of the ancient Greeks. These instruments have limited tonal range and harmonic possibilities. The percussion instruments which presented and marked the rhythmical structure of the Aztec dances were the *huehuetl*, a drum which invited them to the dance, the *panhuehuetl* and the *tlalpanhuehuetl*, which called them to war (which were cylindrical drums of different sizes covered with ocelot skin); the *ayacachtli*, a gourd full of little stones; the *teponaztli*, a sort of xylophone; and the *tzicahuaztli*, a scored femur which was scraped with a stick, and which is today known as a 'güiro'.

With the Conquest in 1521, the era of Hispanic influence begins. The effect on native music was immediate through the introduction of the guitar and other European string instruments. The first school of music was established by Fray Pedro de Gante at Texcoco in 1527. The native boys became skilful musicians and expert in copying the European instruments, and every church had its choir and orchestra. When education conflicted with the interests of the Spaniards, the schools were closed. Music however continued, and the guitar became the popular folk instrument.

Inevitably, a mestizo folk music developed which was a result of the blending of the Spanish and native cultures. The popular expression of this folk music is to be found today in the groups of itinerant musicians known as *mariachis*. It is generally supposed that this is a corruption of the word *mariage*, and derives from the fact that these musicians were frequently employed to play at weddings during the French intervention in Mexico under the Emperor Maximilian. In Mexico City today, the *mariachis* are to be found at the Plaza Garibaldi, from where they are engaged for *gallos* (serenades), and to play at private parties.

The Concheros

Sahagun mentions the amazement shown by the Spaniards at the skill of the Aztecs in the dance. The friars encouraged dancing, and dances were performed on a large scale to dramatise religious teaching. These ritual dances now have nothing religious about them except their intention, and are danced on fiestas or saints' days.

Of the contemporary dancers, the Concheros are the most remarkable, and in the words of one of their songs, they are the 'soldiers of the Conquest of the Holy Religion'. Their name is derived from the instrument most of them play, made from the shell-like covering of the armadillo. They are also called Chichimecas, after a tribe which flourished in the region of Queretaro, and their dances originated among them shortly after the Conquest. When the Chichimecas first began their dances, it may have been to cover up their pagan beliefs and customs, and even today their ceremonies and dances are predominantly pagan.

The Concheros dance regularly at all fiestas, the most important of which are those held at the four cardinal points with respect to Mexico City: La Villa de Guadalupe, Chalma, Los Remedios, and Amecameca. This relationship derives from the ancient worship of the four winds.

The Concheros are organised into military groups under the command of the 'Captain General of the Conquest of the Great Tenochtitlan'. The first captain teaches his soldiers their duties and the dance steps, and is assisted by the second captain, his substitute. The field sergeant is responsible for the behaviour of the soldiers en route to the many fiestas in which they participate. The standard-bearers must take care of their banners; the Malinches* are in charge of the censers, keeping them supplied with incense; and the Devil clears the way for the dancers as well as amusing the spectators.

The costumes are based on primitive dress, and the headdresses are of long, coloured feathers, adorned with mirrors and beads. The men wear wigs of long hair, and the women wear their hair loose. The standards have the images of the saints of the four frontiers in the corners, and are hung with ribbons and sometimes adorned with beads. Before a fiesta, the Concheros gather round a cross and perform their ritual to it, after which they go into the church to pray and dance, and ask permission to perform dances in the atrium.

The Concheros form a circle for their dance, as in ancient times, but instead of accompanying themselves with singing, they now play musical instruments. The dance is begun by the Captain and all the others follow his lead. The dance steps consist of hopping on one foot while making a cross in the air with the other; crossing the feet with a rocking from side to side; jumping on toes; and certain percussive steps.

On leaving a fiesta, the Concheros enter the church to give thanks and take leave of the saint. They dance for days with just a few hours rest for food and drink.

Regional Dances

The present-day regional dances showing the least Spanish influence are those danced by the Yaquis, Mayos, and Tarahumaras, who inhabit parts of the states of Sonora, Sinaloa, Chihuahua, and north-west Durango. The dances are known as Pascolas and Matachines, and they are

* *Malinche:* Spanish corruption of the name Malintzin, the Indian girl who became guide and interpreter to Hernán Cortéz during the Conquest of Mexico. The name has not unnaturally become associated with 'traitor' or 'betrayal to the enemy'.

generally named after animals, so that we find the Venado (deer), Víbora (snake), Tigre (tiger), Coyote, etc. The Pascolas show a pronounced totemic influence, and are danced to instruments called *bules* (gourds filled with small stones), *raspadores* (scored femurs), and *tamborcitos* (small drums), to provide the rhythmic accompaniment, while the melody is played on flutes made of cane reed and on violins. The theme of the Venado is hunting, and the dance imitates the grace and nervousness of the deer, and the triumph of man over animals.

The Pascolas begin to learn to dance at an early age. They have no fear of wild animals, and can imitate every animal to perfection. In their dances, they appear with bare torsos and feet, and around their legs they tie strings of *tenabares* (dried cocoons filled with gravel), and they carry a large gourd rattle in each hand. The dancer imitating the deer wears, in addition, a head-dress of a stuffed deer's head.

The Matachines are ritual dancers in the church organisation who join because of a vow made during illness or for penitence, and call themselves 'Soldiers of the Virgin'. They dance in two lines, making a variety of simple steps and figures. They dance at the funerals of their members and those of their close relatives, and at the church every Sunday; they also take part in the Procession of the Cross in Holy Week. The dances of the Matachines can always be seen at the traditional annual fair of San Marcos in Aguascalientes, and on the day of the Holy Cross in front of the church of San Marcos.

The indigenous Tarahumaras, from the mountains of Chihuahua, dance their own version called Matachin. The Catholic Tarahumaras paint their faces, or use masks representing animals, and go through the streets making people laugh with their extravagant jokes and play acting.

The men and women of the Huasteca Indians, of the state of San Luis Potosí, dance 'Los Matachines'. In Nayarit, Vera Cruz and Coahuila the same type of Matachines are found.

In the region known as the Huasteca, which includes parts of the states of San Luis Potosí, Hidalgo, and Vera Cruz, are to be found the dances called Huapangos. The origin of this name is said to be from *Fandango*, meaning a popular fiesta, although it may be from *Huasteco*, an inhabitant of the region, and *Panuco*, an important river. The dance is performed on a wooden platform, which makes the steps more resonant, by any number of couples. As a sign of prowess, a dancer may carry a tumbler of water on his or her head without spilling a drop. In the well-known Huapango, 'La Bamba', danced especially in the state of Vera Cruz, a scarf is placed on the floor which the dancers tie and untie with their feet while performing a complicated *zapateado*.

Interesting dances are found in the state of Guerrero and include the Machetes, danced by two men and a girl, in which a fight is simulated with *machetes* (very long knives used for cutting sugar cane); the Chilenas, in which women dance with gaily coloured handkerchiefs (a dance probably originating in the Republic of Chile and introduced through the port of Acapulco); and the Tlacololeros, which are dance prayers for food and life. The Tlacololeros are ancient dances, concerned with the hunting of the tiger, in which a dancer, dressed as Death with a scythe, performs a most strange and macabre dance.

The dances of Yucatán, Campeche, Tabasco, and Quintana Roo are known as Jaranas, and are essentially very much like the Spanish Jota. When the Conquistadores introduced the *seguidillas* and *zapateado* into Yucatán, the interpreters of the aboriginal dances soon absorbed the new music, and they combined the new and different musical emotions into the Jarana, which represents the mestizo spirit as do the Jarabe and Huapango. Jarana means 'happy, vivacious'; it is also the name of a five-stringed instrument like a small guitar, from whence the dance derives its name.

The Dances

Abbreviations used in description of steps and dances

r – right ⎫ referring to R – right ⎫ describing turns or
l – left ⎭ hand, foot, etc. L – left ⎭ ground pattern
C – clockwise C-C – counter-clockwise

La Sandunga

The Sandunga (popularly written 'Zandunga') is the regional dance of the Isthmus of Tehuantepec, in the part corresponding to the state of Oaxaca, and is also the name given to the music and to the verses sometimes sung to it. The word Sandunga may be derived from the Zapotec *Saa, Ndu, Nga* (this holy satisfaction), but in Spanish it means 'grace, piquancy, charm'. The origin of the music is not altogether clear; it is perhaps a Zapotec air influenced by the Spanish Fandango, although it is held by some that it is the work of a Tehuantepec composer who was inspired by the death of his mother to write a musical poem of grief. Whatever it may be, the music, played generally on a *marimba*, is unlike any other regional dance and typifies the languorous charm of the Isthmus and the grace and gaiety of the Tehuana women.

The Sandunga is danced at the Isthmus fiestas which are then known as *Velas*, so called because of the elaborately ornamented candles formerly used for illumination. The velas take place on any feast day, such as that held for the patron saint of the town, and also may be organised for any social occasion.

The Tehuanas dance without a smile on their faces and their erect carriage is the result of the custom of carrying

Plate 2 Jarabe Tehuano

baskets and jars on their heads. Their costume is particularly attractive and consists of a loose blouse called a *huipil grande*, cut with a round or square neck, in satin embroidered with flowers. The skirt of satin, embroidered with the same design, is very full and has a flounce of lace about twelve to fifteen inches wide, starched and pleated. The *huipil chico*, which the Tehuanas use as a head-dress, resembles a baby's dress, and the manner in which it is worn indicates whether the dancer is participating in a religious or social function. There are numerous legends connected with the origin of this curious head-dress: in one version, priests' surplices were found in luggage from a shipwreck; while in another, after washing baby clothes in the river these were put on the head, partly to hasten the drying, and partly to keep the head cool! Not the least striking feature of the costume is the jewellery and the habit of wearing on necklaces large gold coins, which form part of the girls' dowry.

The bowl carried on the head is called *jicalpestle* and consists of a large gourd, hollowed and dried, lacquered black, and on which brightly coloured flowers are painted. It is filled with fruit and flowers and is adorned with paper flags cut in a lace-like pattern.

Although the Sandunga is considered a dance for women, men do participate, when the version is somewhat different. Their costume consists of white trousers, loose white shirt and a straw hat; some wear *huaraches* (sandals). But the girls always dance barefooted.

Region Isthmus of Tehuantepec, especially Yucatán and Tehuantepec in the state of Oaxaca.

Character Dignified and graceful. The dancers perform without smiling, as it is in the nature of a religious dance. The style throughout is natural, with the body held quietly erect.

Formation Sixteen girls enter to perform in a square.

Dance

The girls enter holding their bowls on their heads, those on R using l hand and *vice versa*. To gather the skirt in other hand, let the arm hang down by the side, body erect. Then, in the position where the hand falls, pick up the skirt, and rest back of the hand on the waist at the side, the palm outwards.

$$\underbrace{8\ 7\ 6\ 5}_{\downarrow}\ \underbrace{4\ 3\ 2\ 1}_{\downarrow}\ \underbrace{1\ 2\ 3\ 4}_{\downarrow}\ \underbrace{5\ 6\ 7\ 8}_{\downarrow}$$

	MUSIC
STEP 1	*Bars*
After Introductory bar, the girls begin on bar 1, taking 32 steps to reach their position for Step 2.	
Take a fairly short step on to whole l foot (*one*), and circle the r foot up, round and forwards (*two, three*), before putting it down for the next step. The moving foot is held naturally, not over-stretched at the instep, and the knee in a natural line forwards.	1–16
Repeat.	1–16

STEP 2

The girls have reached their positions of 4 square.

```
8 4 4 8
7 3 3 7
6 2 2 6
5 1 1 5
```

In place. Step on l foot, flat (*one*); give a slight hop, lifting r foot just in front of l ankle (*two*); put r foot down beside l (*three*).	17
Repeat five more times with same foot.	18–22
Four alternate stamps on to whole foot, l, r, l and r foot.	23–24
In performing the stamps, lift the foot a little backwards, bending the knee, and bring it forwards with the stamp. The knees slightly bent.	
Repeat on other foot (as from bar 17).	25–32
Repeat whole Step.	17–(32)

STEP 3

This Step is performed in couples. In the front line, numbers 5 & 1 work together; in the second, 6 & 2, and so on for every line. Facing the front, the partner on L always passes behind on the crossing steps. Partners on L start with r foot; those on R with l foot.

The step, Balancé, is a waltz step in place, in a natural manner, the feet straight, and with scarcely any rise and fall, and no side sway, of body.

Balancé r, l, r turning about 1/8 of a turn towards partner.	33

SANDUNGA

Arranged by Guillermina Dickins

(Play first time as written. After D.C., play A A, B, A ,C C)

Balancé l, r, l turning about 1/8 of a turn away from partner.	34
Cross over in three steps: r foot (*one, two*) l foot (*three*), r foot (*one, two, three*). Turn once round while crossing.	35–36
Repeat on other foot. Return to own places.	37–40
Repeat the Step again.	41–48

STEP 4

Stamp r foot flat (*one*); place l foot on ball beside r foot (*two*); slight stamp of l foot on ball about the distance of half a foot to side of r foot (*three*).	33–40
On the first two beats, the weight of the body moves the r hip over to the r side, and on the 3rd beat the l hip follows the weight of the body as it is partly taken on to l foot. The movement is very slight, and the steps very small. There is no rise and fall, the head and the body from the waist upwards remain quite steady. This step is done six times, making a half turn to R, finishing with back to the audience.	
Return to face the front, making a half turn to L with four alternate stamps, l, r, l, r, as performed in Step 2.	
Repeat, beginning on l foot, turning to L.	41–(48)

STEP 5

In place. Stand still, feet together. Bend body forwards as the bowl is lowered to the ground in front. In bending, the knees are kept almost straight, just bending a little to give grace. The dancers straighten up and pick up their skirts with both hands at the sides, to show the ankles, on the last two bars.	1–8
	9–16

STEP 6

The girls circle round their bowls doing the same slightly springing waltz step and moving their skirts from side to side (hands move to R on the waltz step beginning with r foot) in a natural manner. There is no side-to-side body sway. Dancers, always facing front, do eight waltz steps C then eight waltz steps C-C round bowls.

1–16

STEP 7

All the girls move together in the following manner, always facing front, with the same waltz step. No. 1 replaces No. 4 and No. 4 replaces No. 1 taking eight waltz steps C-C. Nos. 2 & 3 also move C-C in a full circle to return to original places.

17–24

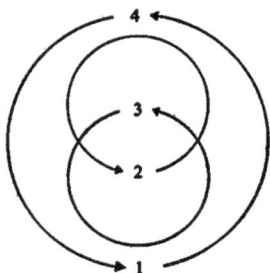

Then, moving in the same direction, they all assume original positions. (They all move their skirts as they dance, as in previous Steps.)

25–32

STEP 8

They now make two big circles. The eight dancers on R move C, the eight on L move C-C with eight waltz steps. But this time the Step is performed moving forwards with longer steps. On each step the feet pass, moving forwards. The skirts are moved from side to side as before. Do not sway body.
Repeat, reversing the direction.

1–8

9–16

STEP 9

They pick up their bowls in the same manner as they put them down, keeping their feet together and bending the body forwards, taking eight bars to place the bowls on their heads. The girls in the two columns on R hold the bowls with r hand, and hold skirts away from the body with l hand. Girls in the other two columns use the reverse hands.

33–40

STEP 10

The eight girls on L start on l foot; those on R on r foot. The two inside columns (Nos. 1 to 4) move forward in front of Nos. 5 to 8, who

41–48

```
            8 4 4 8
            7 3 3 7
            6 2 2 6
            5 1 1 5
  1 2 3 4   | |   4 3 2 1
←                         →
```

then join on to their respective lines in same order as they entered. They all exit eight to each side with a waltz step, moving forward, and waving their skirts across the front and out to the side, with the hand nearest the audience.
Repeat music, if desired, from bar 33. 33-47 (continuing into 49)

Los Viejitos (The Little Old Men)

This dance of the Purépecha Indians is undoubtedly the most original and characteristic of the state of Michoacán. It has a strong comic feeling in spite of its religious intention. The dance groups are made up of twelve to twenty dancers and the director is the one who plays the *Jarana*, a stringed instrument used to accompany the dance. The choreography and the general representation of the dancers depend upon the artistic refinement of the dance director. They wear a palm hat with a very low, round crown and a broad brim trimmed with emerald green, bright purple, and red ribbons that hang down four or five inches from the brim. They cover the head with a white cloth and cactus fibres are attached at the edge of the mask, to suggest a wig. The masks have a strong expression of laughter or sadness, and are made principally in Santa Fé de la Laguna. They wear round the collar a red handkerchief, a poncho of a bright colour, and white trousers with twelve inches of embroidery at the bottom. Around the waist a long red sash is sometimes worn trimmed with a fringe on the ends. Their *huanengo* (a kind of blanket) is embroidered with beautiful cross-stitch patterns of red wool, although some dancers may use only a grey or red *gabancito* (a thin plain blanket). The sandals are strong, in black or brown and with a back. The dancers carry a cane in the right hand, roughly carved with an animal figure on the handle.

Headed by the director of the dance, the rest make their entrance in a single file. Durán writes, 'There was another dance of *viejos* danced with masks of old men and humpbacked; it lacked grace but was gay and very funny'. The dance is executed by boys, with quick, nimble steps and much shaking in imitation of old men. It is commonly believed that this is a totemic dance, in which the spirits of old age are to be discouraged by seeing active old men.

Region	Michoacán, especially in the villages round Lake Pátzcuaro.
Character	A rapid dance with much shaking to imitate old age.
Formation	Twelve to twenty boys.

Dance

The dancers enter from R, or L, in a file, one behind the other, holding their canes (pointing downwards) in both hands in front of them. The director leads with his *Jarana*. They move across, without music, to form a straight line, taking the equivalent of 12 bars of 6/8 time.

STEP 1	MUSIC *Bars*
The step used is a very quick stamping of the feet in a triple-count rhythm, with the accent on the first step of each triple count. Dancers bend forward over their sticks, shaking their shoulders and bodies.	
a Stamp l foot flat, l heel just in front of r foot (*one*). Stamp r foot flat, in place (*and*). Stamp l foot flat, joining it to r foot ('*a*').	equi- valent of half a bar
Repeat, starting with r foot (*two & a*). Repeat, starting with l foot (*three & a*). Repeat, starting with r foot (*four & a*). Repeat, starting with l foot (*five & a*). Repeat, starting with r foot (*six & a*). Four alternate stamps on the whole foot with feet together, l, r, l (*seven & a*), r (*eight & a*). Repeat the whole from the beginning and at the end of the four stamps, face the front.	
b Then do the triple counts twice more, on the spot, or moving very slightly forwards, l, r, l (*one & a*); r, l, r (*two & a*); four alternate	

stamps, as before, l, r, l (*three & a*); r (*four &a*).
Repeat again from *b* and on the last stamp (r foot) the music strikes the first chord of Introductory bar.

STEP 2

The cane is held, point on the floor, with both hands. All dancers bend over canes and face the audience in one line.

Beat ball of r foot, the knee and toe turned inwards, the foot placed sideways (*one*). | 1

Join r foot to l, heels together, feet flat, toes out (*& a*).

Beat ball of l foot to side, foot and knee turned in (*two*).

Join l foot to r, feet flat, heels together, toes out (*& a*).

Repeat with r foot (*one & a*). | 2
Repeat with l foot (*two & a*).
Bend both knees, knees and toes inwards, heels raised (*one*). | 3

Put heels down, knees bent, heels together, toes outwards (*& a*).

Keeping knees bent, raise heels, toes and knees outwards (*two*).

Put heels down again, knees bent, feet together (*& a*).

Repeat bar 3. | 4
Repeat (as from bars 1 to 4) three times. | 5–16

STEP 3: THE 'OCÓN'

Stamp l foot flat (*one*). | 17
Beat r heel (toe slightly raised) on ground just behind l heel (*and*).
Hop on l foot ('*a*').
Beat r heel again as before (*two*).

Hop on l foot again (*and*).	
Stamp r foot flat (*one*).	18
Beat l heel just behind r heel (*and*).	
Hop on r foot ('*a*').	
Beat l heel again as before (*two*).	
Hop on r foot (*and*).	
Repeat, starting on l foot (as bar 17).	19
Stamp r foot, flat, beside l and hold it (*one & two*).	20
Repeat the whole again from bars 17 to 20.	17–20

STEP 4

Move forward for eight bars, knees bent all the time. Shake whole body to imitate old age.	
Put r foot forward, a short step, on ball of foot (*one & a*).	21
Let r heel drop, knees still bent (*two & a*).	
Repeat same with l foot.	22
Repeat with alternate feet to bar 28.	23–28
Repeat with same steps moving backwards.	21–28

STEP 5

Repeat Step 3: The 'Ocón'.	29–32 twice

STEP 6

Move once round stationary cane, C, with the following step (counting 6 beats for music):	
Stamp l foot, flat, taking weight (*one*).	33
Brush-beat r heel forward (no weight) (*two*).	
Bring r foot back beside l foot, taking weight on to ball (*three*). N.B. Do not let body rise.	
Repeat with the same foot (*four, five, six*).	
Repeat twice more with the same foot.	34
Then, having arrived back in place, to face front, do five quick alternate stamps with foot flat, l,r,l,r,l (*one, two, three, four, five*) pause (*six*).	35

Repeat five quick stamps r, l, r, l, r, pause (*six*).	36
Repeat entire Step (as from bar 33). Begin with same foot and move C-C round cane.	37–40
If desired, the whole Step can be repeated.	33–40

STEP 7

Repeat Step 3: The 'Ocón'.	41–44 twice

STEP 8

Holding cane with both hands, point on floor, (counting six beats for the music) jump feet apart moving forward (*one, two, three*).* Jump feet together (*four, five, six*).	45
Two jumps forward with feet together (half bar to each jump).	46
Repeat the jump feet apart and together.	47
Repeat the two jumps feet together.	48
Then repeat the whole Step (as from bar 45) but moving backward.	49–52

*The 'even' dancers start moving forward, the 'odd' backward. They reverse on last four bars.

STEP 9

Repeat Step 3: The 'Ocón'.	53–56 twice

STEP 10

Exit in a file, as they entered, knees bent and shaking whole body as they go (music 3/4).

Stamp ball of r foot forward, knees bent (*one*). Let heel of r foot drop, knees bent (*two*). Stamp ball of l foot forward (*three*). Let heel of l foot drop (*one*). Stamp ball of r foot forward (*two*). Let heel of r foot drop (*three*). Repeat alternate feet till all dancers are off.	57–64
(Repeat music, if necessary, for all to exit.)	57–64

LOS VIEJITOS

Arranged by Guillermina Dickins

Jarabe Tapatío

The Jarabe Tapatío is perhaps the best known and most popular of all Mexican dances. G. Baqueiro Foster, the eminent Mexican musicologist, distinguishes three groups of Jarabe, a generic name for a combination of *sones* or popular melodies: those derived from the *seguidillas*, the *boleras*; those from the *bolero*; and those from the *fandango* and the Spanish *zapateado*. The most characteristic and authentic forms are the Jarabe Tehuano; the Jarabe del Sotavento, from Vera Cruz; and the Jarabes of Yucatán and Tabasco. The national dance of Mexico, the so-called Jarabe Tapatío, is not really a true Jarabe since it cannot be said to be derived from these sources.

The Jarabe Tapatío was first danced in its present form at the Coliseo in Mexico City, July 9th 1790. It was then performed by a Spanish clown in a travesty of women's clothes. These Jarabes rapidly caught the public fancy, so that in 1802 the dance was forbidden by the Viceroy, Don Felix Berenguer, because of the indecent words sung to accompany it. The Jarabe Tapatío was revived before the court of Maximilian and Carlota, and became especially popular with the high society of Guadalajara. The people of Guadalajara are called Tapatíos, and from this the dance was named.

Although most of the steps are obviously derived from Spanish dances, it is also possible to identify steps of Mexican origin, such as those imitating the prance of a horse (since horses played an important part in the Conquest and caused a profound impression on the Aztecs) and those at the end of the dance imitating the courtship of doves.

The costumes used are the *China Poblana* for the girl, and the *Charro* for the boy. The Charro wears long, tight fitting trousers made of chamois leather or of wool material, the full length of the outside of the leg decorated with silver buttons or gold leaves; a white shirt and a silk necktie tied in a bow, a waistcoat and jacket of chamois leather or wool embroidered on the back and lapels, in front and on the arms. He normally wears a leather belt that holds a pistol. Flung over his shoulder is his *sarape*, a brightly coloured woven blanket. He also wears the typical wide-brimmed hat, or *sombrero*, made out of a heavy felt and embroidered to match the suit with silver or gold thread in the shape of roses. He always keeps his hands clasped behind his back, holding his pistol, a gesture of respect to the girl which springs from old Aztec and Spanish traditions.

The origin of the costume known as the China Poblana, is one of Mexico's most charming legends. In one of the versions she is a Mongolian princess who was brought to Acapulco as a slave, and sold to a distinguished family of Puebla who adopted her as a daughter. She was much admired for her virtue and charity, and her richly embroidered costume was widely imitated. When she died, in memory of her kindness, the costume was named after her: *china* (chinese or oriental) *poblana* (from Puebla).

The blouse is of white linen with a square neck and has short sleeves. It is trimmed around the neck and down the front with embroidery of bright coloured silk thread, or tiny glass beads. The skirt is called *zagalejo*, and is made of material called *castor*. This is covered with varicoloured sequins, and the hem is edged with a three-inch band of bright green or red satin. The top of the skirt has set-in points of the same material. A bright coloured *rebozo* (a kind of shawl) is wound around the waist, crossed over the back, with each end brought forward over the shoulders and tucked under itself at the waist. The shoes are high-heeled, bright red or green, and a white starched petticoat, trimmed with lace is worn under the skirt. Hair is parted in the centre, and braided into two plaits which are tied with ribbons of the national colours, red, white and green.

Region   The national dance throughout Mexico.

Character   A dance of courtship and flirtation.

Formation   This dance is performed by couples; the boy is very gallant and the girl very coquettish.

Dance

The musician plays a long chord while the 'charro' holding the 'china's' l hand in his r, comes running in (preferably from L). He whirls her round by releasing her hand and flinging her away from him. She runs (turning round to her L) with small quick steps, gives a half turn and faces the man on the finish of the chord.

STEP I	MUSIC
Both dancers incline the body forward from the hips, keeping the knees rather relaxed. The girl holds her skirt with both hands in front, raising it a little to show the lace on her petticoat; the boy keeps his hands clasped behind his back. They move forward to meet each other with the following movements:	*Bars*
Place r foot forward, taking weight on heel, toe off ground (*one*).	1–8
Slight stamp with ball of l foot, in place, taking weight (*two*).	
Bring r foot back and stamp ball of foot beside l foot, both knees still slightly bent (*three*).	
Repeat with l foot (*four, five, six*).	
Repeat the same movements, starting alternately r and l foot for seven more bars. They meet centre, r shoulder to r shoulder, on the 8th bar and, turning their faces over their r shoulders to look at each other, lift l foot backwards, from the knee, and stamp it strongly beside r foot.	

Plate 3 Jarabe Tapatio

JARABE TAPATIO

Arranged by Guillermina Die

34

They continue in the same direction – away from one another – for the repeat of the music, turning to R, with a stamp, to face each other, in each other's places on bar (8).	1–(8)

There is no 'rise and fall' of the body in this Step. The head is kept 'level', and the shoulders still, the feet move very quickly 'under the body' in small steps, the knees remaining slightly bent throughout. On each triple-count step the girl moves her skirt slightly from side to side (to r side with r foot forward), the movement coming from wrists, the upper arm kept rather still.

STEP 2

(Boy is now on R, girl on L.)
This is the same as Step 1 with a stamp and 'pull-back' added.

Stamp l foot flat, full weight, knee slightly bent (*one*).	9

Pull l foot back on floor, flat, by straightening knee, the body inclined forward (*two*).

Stamp r foot forward on heel, toe lifted, taking weight (*three*).

Stamp ball of l foot in place, taking weight (*four*).

Bring r foot back, on ball of foot, beside l, taking weight (*five*).

Pause (*six*).

Repeat the whole Step always with l foot, seven more times to meet C.	10–16

The steps are very quick, small, and 'level' except for the 'pull-back', which gives a slight jerk. Keep body inclined forward throughout.

Dancers continue and, passing r shoulders, they change places.	9–(16)

STEP 3
(Boy is now on L, girl on R.)
Repeat Step 1, but eliminating the stamp and turn of face in the centre, crossing to opposite places in eight bars. | 17–24

STEP 4 (Music in 3/4 time)
The dancers do three big prancing steps:
Spring on to r foot, raising l thigh to hip level, knee slightly bent. | 25
Spring on to l foot, raising r thigh to hip level, knee slightly bent.
Spring on to r foot, raising l thigh to hip level, knee slightly bent.
They meet centre where they cross l foot over r, bending knees well, and letting *left* shoulder drop. Bend the body, looking over shoulder at partner, turning once round to R, the weight on balls of both feet. | 26
As they again face each other they straighten body and legs.
Repeat the same steps and the turn to R, continuing in same direction, changing to opposite places. | 27–28
In place, they turn to L with three 'pivots' on the spot, i.e. stamp with weight on l foot (*one*), take weight on to ball of r foot (*and*). Repeat twice l – r (*two and*), l – r (*three and*). | 29
Step on to l foot, facing partner (*one*); stamp r foot beside l foot (*two*); pause (*three*). | 30
Repeat the three 'pivots' turning to R on r foot. | 31
Step on to r foot and stamp l foot beside r. | 32
Repeat the movements as for bars 29 to 32. | 33–36
Repeat the whole Step. | 25–(36)

STEP 5

(Boy is now on R, girl on L.) The dancers change to opposite places. They should always pass with the same shoulder.

With a jump throw weight on to r foot, diagonally forward, moving the body so that r shoulder follows r foot obliquely forward to R. Leave l leg straight, foot off ground behind (*one*).   37

Slide l foot, crossing it behind r, taking weight on to ball of foot, rising and beginning to change direction of body sway (*two*).

Bring r foot back beside l, letting r shoulder swing gently backward to follow r leg (*three*).

Repeat, starting on l foot.   38
Repeat twice more with r and l foot.   39–40
Now in opposite places, they cross the r foot over in front of l, and do twelve 'rocks' forward on to r foot and back on to l, turning round to their L, and finishing facing each other.   41–44

Repeat the whole Step.   37–(44)

STEP 6 (Music in 6/8 time)

(Boy is now on R, girl on L.)
Repeat Step 2 to meet in the centre.   45–52
Repeat, to cross to opposite sides. Again pass r shoulders.   45–(52)

STEP 7 (Music in 2/4 time)

(Boy is now on L, girl on R.)
Both facing the front, they move to centre with four sideways gallops (2 gallops to one bar). The boy uses r foot to step to side, and closes l. The girl uses l foot to side, and closes r.   53–54

The 'charro' attempts to kiss girl, who turns   55

her face away, covering it with her arm.	
They return to their places (boy to L, girl to R) with four gallops.	56–57
Turn to face each other.	58
On repeat of music they take four walking steps to meet centre – r, l, r, l.	53–54
Two steps turning to R as they meet, r, l.	55
Four walks, continuing in same direction to opposite places.	56–57
Turn with a stamp to face each other.	(58)
From bars 56–(58) the 'charro' takes off his hat and flings it on the floor in the direction of his partner.	
Both dance towards the hat as follows:	
Stamp r foot forward (*one*).	59
Stamp ball of l foot behind (*and*).	
Stamp r foot in front (*two*).	
Slide (brush) l foot forward (*and*).	
Repeat starting with l foot.	60
Repeat six more times with alternate feet.	61–66
With a jump the girl crosses r foot over l foot, weight on toes, and shifts her weight from one foot to the other, bending knees and ankles a little (i.e. rocks foot to foot), going round the outside of brim of hat, C. (Do two 'rocks' to one bar.) At the same time the boy goes round the hat C-C. His step is similar, but larger. With a jump he throws his weight on r foot, moving body obliquely, then slides l foot behind. He looks at her the whole time, trying to catch her eyes. He moves outside the girl.	67–74
The next three bars are played very slowly – like five slow chords.	
The girl kneels, bending very low. The boy whirls his r leg over her and she picks up the hat with both hands. She gets up, and the two	75–77

stand side by side, facing front, the girl on the R, holding the hat on her head with both hands, the boy with r arm round her waist.

STEP 8

a They do four skips, r, l, r, l forward (one skip to one bar).	78–81
b Spring on l foot, putting r heel forward on ground, toe raised.	82
Spring on l foot, putting r toe on ground in front of l toe, r knee bent and a little turned out.	83
Spring on l foot, placing r heel on ground to the side.	84
Spring and close r foot to L.	85
c Four skips backward l, r, l, r.	78–81
Repeat *b* springing on r foot.	82–85
Repeat *a*, *b*, *c*, *b*.	86–101
Sixteen big jumps in place, alternately raising l and r leg in front, knee straight, the foot of raised leg about level with knee of supporting leg. Take one bar to each spring.	102–117
Boy takes his arm away from his partner's waist. Both put r foot across over l in making a full turn to L. The 'charro' kneels on his l knee, holding the 'china's' l hand, while she places her l foot on his thigh.	118–119

Plate 4 *La Sandunga*

Bibliography

CAMPOS, RUBEN M. – *El Folklore y la Musica Mexicana.* Secretaría Educación Pública, Mexico, D.F. 1928.

CLAVIJERO, FRANCISCO. – *Historia Antigua de Méjico.* Mexico, 1927. (Al in English.)

COVARRUBIAS, MIGUEL. – *Mexico South, The Isthmus of Tehuantep* Cassell, London, 1945; Knopf, New York, 1946.

DIAZ DEL CASTILLO, BERNAL. – *Discovery and Conquest of Mexico 1517–152* Translated with an introduction and notes by A. P. Maudsla Harper, New York, 1928; Routledge, London.

DURAN, FRAY DIEGO. – *Historia de las Indias de Nueva España.* Mexic 1880.

LUMHOLTZ, CARL. – *Unknown Mexico.* Scribner, New York, 1902; Ma millan, London, 1903.

MONTES DE OCA, JOSE G. – *Danzas Indígenas Mejicanas.* Imprenta d Estado de Tlaxcala, Mexico, 1926.

OROZCO, GILBERTO. – *Tradiciones y Leyendas del Istmo de Tehuantep* Revista Musical Mexicana, Mexico, D.F. 1946.

PRESCOTT, WILLIAM H. – *Conquest of Mexico.*

SAHAGUN, FRAY BERNADINO. – *Historia General de las Cosas de Nue España.* Mexico. 5 volumes. (Portions have been translated in English and published by Fisk University, U.S.A., 1938.)

TOOR, FRANCES. – *A Treasury of Mexican Folkways.* Crown Publishe New York, 1947.

VASQUEZ SANTA ANA, HIGINIO. – *Fiestas y Costumbres Mejicanas.* Edicion Botas. Mexico, 1940.

VARIOUS PAMPHLETS: Compiled from field research on Mexican danc Dirección de Misiones Culturales, Secretaría de Educación Públic Mexico, D.F.

www.ingramcontent.com/pod-product-compliance
Lightning Source LLC
Chambersburg PA
CBHW061743290426

43661CB00127B/963